Nicola Moon

Planets

Illustrated by Rob Jakeway

OXFORD
UNIVERSITY PRESS

This book belongs to

OXFORD
UNIVERSITY PRESS

Great Clarendon Street, Oxford OX2 6DP

Oxford University Press is a department of the University of Oxford.
It furthers the University's objective of excellence in research, scholarship,
and education by publishing worldwide in

Oxford New York

Auckland Bangkok Buenos Aires Cape Town Chennai
Dar es Salaam Delhi Hong Kong Istanbul Karachi Kolkata
Kuala Lumpur Madrid Melbourne Mexico City Mumbai Nairobi
São Paulo Shanghai Singapore Taipei Tokyo Toronto

First published 2002

Paperback ISBN 0–19–910749–1

3 5 7 9 10 8 6 4 2

Printed in Spain by Edelvives

Contents

► Voyage into space

ZOOOOOOM!

Hold tight as our spaceship flies through space! Look down there – where are we?

That is the planet Mercury, the first stop on our journey. Mercury is the planet nearest to the sun. Let's orbit round a few times.

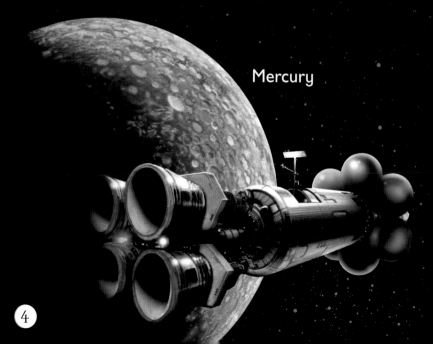

Mercury

From Mercury the sun looks enormous in the jet-black sky. This is a grey world, with dusty plains, high cliffs and huge craters.

It's not safe to land the spaceship. There's no air out there, and it's **HOT!** Hotter than the hottest oven. A pizza would burn to a crisp in seconds!

But at night it will get really **COLD.** Much colder than ice.

Altogether there are nine planets circling our sun. They are:

One way to remember the planets in the right order is to make up a sentence using the first letters. Here's an example:

Many Very Excited Mammoths Jumping and Skipping Uphill in New Pyjamas.

Perhaps you could make up your own sentence?

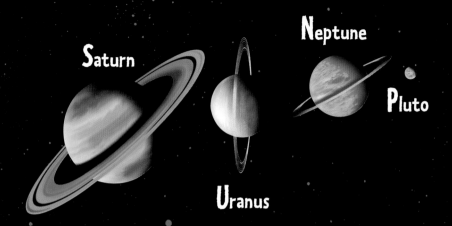

Saturn

Uranus

Neptune

Pluto

A real journey to visit all the planets would take many years. By the time we returned you would be grown up!

Luckily, we can pretend. Which planet is next to Mercury?

Did you know...
A planet is a big ball of rock or gas that orbits the sun. As the planet travels it spins like a top. The time it takes for a planet to spin round once is the length of one day for that planet.

▶ Beautiful Venus

Look! There's Venus!

It looks beautiful with its cream-coloured clouds, but it is a very scary place. Down under those pretty clouds it is hot enough to melt metal, and it is impossible to breathe.

Drops of acid, strong enough to eat through rock, fall from the clouds. Thunder roars and lightning flashes in the orange sky, and there are thousands of volcanoes!

surface of Venus

The force of those pretty clouds pressing down on Venus is enough to crush a car – easily! Try putting your hand inside a rubber glove, then hold it under water. Can you feel the force of the water pressing on the glove? That is how the clouds press down on Venus – but MUCH harder!

Did you know...
On Venus the sun rises in the west and sets in the east. This is the opposite to what happens on Earth. It happens because Venus spins in the opposite direction to Earth.

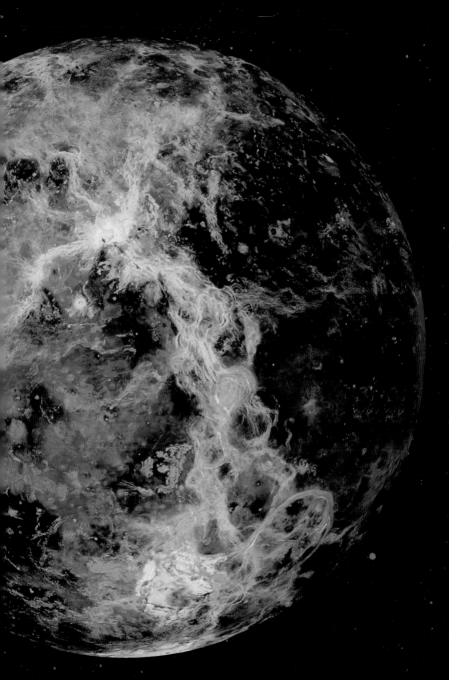

Venus beneath the clouds

▶ Home, sweet home

Now we are passing a beautiful planet. Do you recognize it? That is our Earth!

Earth is the only one of the nine planets where there are plants and animals. That is because it is just the right distance from the sun. It is not too hot and not too cold. There is plenty of water, and air that we can breathe.

But it's not time to go home yet. There are more planets to see!

▶ The red planet

The next planet is Mars. Why do you think it is called the red planet?

The surface of Mars is like a cold, dry desert. There are rocks and boulders everywhere, and the ground is covered with red dust. There are huge mountains and deep valleys, and the sky looks pink.

surface of Mars

There are marks on the ground that look like river beds. Perhaps millions of years ago there were rivers on Mars, but now it is completely dry. And freezing. **Brrrrrr!**

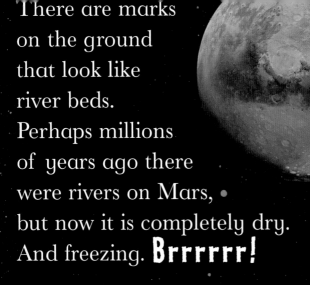

Luckily we can keep warm inside our spaceship as we head for another planet.

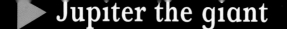

Jupiter the giant

Wow! Look at that! It's **ENORMOUS!**

Jupiter is the biggest planet. It is so big that more than 1000 planets the size of Earth could fit inside it. Jupiter is made of gas, so there is no solid surface to land on, even if we wanted to.

surface of Jupiter

Look at the orange, brown and red clouds, swirling and changing all the time. Do you see the red spot on Jupiter? The spot is a very violent storm, like a tornado.

Gales and hurricanes blow here all the time, and it is very cold. Much colder than inside a deep freeze. Let's go!

Did you know...
Jupiter spins faster than any other planet. A day on Jupiter is only ten hours long!

Rings round Saturn

The next planet is Saturn. It's easy to recognize because of those broad, bright rings.

Saturn's rings

Scientists think the rings are made of lumps of ice and rock. Some of the lumps are as big as houses, others as small as dust, circling Saturn like a blizzard.

Saturn looks very peaceful with its
creamy yellow clouds, but sometimes
there are sudden storms with winds
blowing over 1000 miles per hour.
Enough to
blow your
house across
the town!

Did you know...
Saturn has eighteen
moons. Our planet
Earth only has one.

Saturn and two
of its moons

▶ The faraway planets

As we speed further into space the
sun looks smaller and smaller.
Because the sun is so far away it is
very cold out here.

the sun

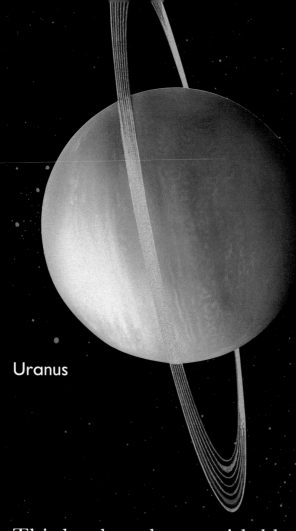

Uranus

This lovely pale greenish-blue planet is Uranus. Have you noticed that it spins on its side? It means that while one half of Uranus has 42 years of daylight, the other half has 42 years of darkness. Can you imagine that?

The next planet is spinning the right way up! Neptune is as blue as the ocean, with clouds and swirling tornadoes. One Neptune year is as long as 165 Earth years. Longer than anyone on Earth has ever lived!

Neptune

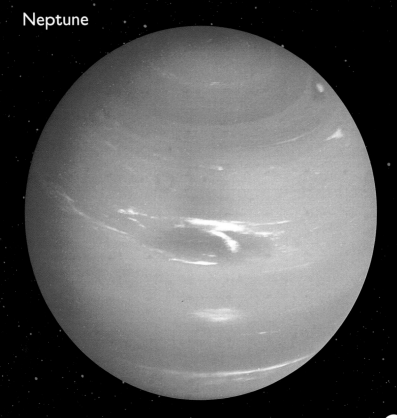

The last planet is Pluto, the smallest planet. There it is, far away in the distance. It's a tiny world of rock and ice – or so scientists believe. Pluto is so far away that no spacecraft has ever seen it close up. Perhaps one day, when you have grown up, scientists will know more.

Pluto and its moon

▶ The return journey

Before we go, look out at all those
stars twinkling in the darkness.
Did you know that our sun is a star,
just like billions of others?

Maybe some of those other stars could have planets circling around them. And one of those planets could be just the right distance from its star to have water and air. And maybe, just maybe, there could be life on that planet, just like on Earth. Think of that, next time you gaze up at the sky on a starry night!

As we head back home to Earth, we zoom past the planets once again. Can you recognize this one?

Now our journey's nearly over.
Hold tight! We're going to land – in
the ocean…

SPLOSH!

▶ Planet facts

Below is a table of things you might like to know about the planets.

	Mercury	Venus	Earth	Mars
Length of day*	59 days	243 days	24 hours	24 hours 37 minutes
Length of year*	88 days	225 days	365 days	687 days
Average Temperature	427°C day -170°C night	480°C	22°C	-23°C
Air we can breathe	no	no	yes	no
Water	no	no	yes	no
Number of moons	0	0	1	2
Distance from sun (million km)	58	108	150	228
Relative size	orange pip	small grape	grape	pea

*Earth days/hours/minutes)

Remember, a day is the length of time it takes a planet to spin round once. A year is the length of time it takes for a planet to travel round the sun.

Jupiter	Saturn	Uranus	Neptune	Pluto
10 hours	10 hours 14 minutes	17 hours 54 minutes	19 hours 12 minutes	6 days
12 years	29 years	84 years	165 years	248 years
-150°C	-180°C	-210°C	-220°C	-230°C
no	no	no	no	no
no	no	no	no	no
16	18	15	8	1
778	1,427	2,869	4,496	5,900
small melon	grapefruit	lime	tomato	peppercorn

▶ Glossary

This glossary will help you to understand what some important words mean. You can find them in this book by using the page numbers given below.

acid An acid is a sort of chemical. Strong acids are so dangerous they can burn your skin or eat into rock. **9**

crater A crater is a big hole which has been made by something heavy hitting the ground. **5**

gas Gas is like air. It can move about to fill up any space. Many gases are invisible, but some are coloured, and some are smelly. **7, 16**

moon A moon is a ball of rock that circles round a planet. Earth has one moon, which you can see in the sky at night. **20, 28**

orbit An orbit is the invisible path travelled by a planet as it circles the sun. We can say that a planet orbits the sun. **4, 7**

star A star is a big ball of hot, glowing gas in space. Stars give out light and heat. You can see them twinkling in the sky at night. **25, 26**

sun The sun is a star. It's nearer to Earth than any other star. It gives us warmth and light.
4, 5, 6, 7, 11, 13, 21, 25, 28, 29

tornado A tornado is a very strong wind that whirls round in circles. **17, 23**

Reading Together

Oxford Reds have been written by leading children's authors who have a passion for particular non-fiction subjects. So as well as up-to-date information, fascinating facts and stunning pictures, these books provide powerful writing which draws the reader into the text.

Oxford Reds are written in simple language, checked by educational advisors. There is plenty of repetition of words and phrases, and all technical words are explained. They are an ideal vehicle for helping your child develop a love of reading – by building fluency, confidence and enjoyment.

You can help your child by reading the first few pages out loud, then encourage him or her to continue alone. You could share the reading by taking turns to read a page or two. Or you could read the whole book aloud, so your child knows it well before tackling it alone.

Oxford Reds will help your child develop a love of reading and a lasting curiosity about the world we live in.

Sue Palmer
Writer and Literacy Consultant